Uploaded ▶

20 Ways to Make Your YouTube Channel stand out

Sean Worth

This book is dedicated to my sister Emily who helped design the cover and page layout, love you!

INTRODUCTION

I have always loved technology, we had an old iMac when I was little. I was constantly playing computer games on it. One day in 2009, my dad let me create an account on his PC. After that, I was always on it. I would plug headphones into it and just sit on the couch playing with the webcam until my mom said dinner was ready. I was really into the webcam programs like CyberLink YouCam. I would create short, dumb videos with MANY effects. Then, I found Windows Movie Maker and I just started making my own videos. It was awesome when I figured out how to burn DVDs in the computer. I would make around 5 DVDs a day on just random YouTube or home videos.

I discovered YouTube in around 2007 when my mom was watching a video of someone doing a prank call. I asked her what website was she on and she said it was YouTube. I loved the name and it made me imagine myself looking through a cardboard tube for some reason.

I started watching videos on YouTube and in February 2011, I made my own channel. It was called TheSongsInstrumental and I was basically going to play karaoke songs and rock out to them, Unfortunately, no one wanted to see that (surprisingly.) That channel remained inactive for a 2 years while I was figuring out what to do on YouTube. I just couldn't find that one thing that I truly wanted to do.

One Tuesday night. I was outside picking up sticks, for some reason, when it hit me, "I will do product reviews on YouTube!" I thought it was a good idea because we had so many tech products and games. In 2012, I started messing with a Mac Mini that we had. We put it in my room and I bought a horrible Microsoft webcam. I started something called SeanViews on February 5, 2013. I first made a review of Just Dance. I started getting into it and made videos almost every week. Sometimes I wasn't very consistent with them. (One review was made in May, the next in December!)

I started making "Seasons" of SeanViews. I wanted to make a new intro and new setup every season to keep things fresh. I really wasn't very popular, obviously. My main influence for making videos was iJustine. I loved watching her and she seemed like she had so much fun making her videos. I wanted to be a part of that. She was my internet mentor.

2 months after I debuted SeanViews, I made a new channel so I could get rid of TheSongsInstrumental (which is still my SeanViews Extras channel.) I made the username seanviewsoffical. I didn't realize that I spelled the word official wrong until after I published it and couldn't change it. Last year, I was able to get it changed so my username is now just "seanviews." I don't make reviews very often anymore but I will still occasionally make one. I have moved my channel to bigger and better things.

I decided to create this book as a guide to anyone who wants to start a YouTube channel. I aspire to make this something that would have helped me incredibly when I started my channel. This book will be divided into 6 different parts, all filled with tips and tricks that I have picked up over my 4 years of making videos. I really hope you enjoy it, and thanks for taking the time to read it.

-Sean

STARTING your channel

1 DESIGN CHANNEL ART

A channel banner is one of the first things someone will see when they go to your channel. You will want to make it eye-catching. If you aren't very good with graphics, there are plenty of affordable, freelance graphic designers you can reach out to. The banner should say the name of your channel, maybe the kind of videos you make, and an upload schedule ("New Videos Every Friday," for example). Look around at other YouTubers' channel art for inspiration; many use bright colors to catch viewers' attention. The resolution of your images is very important. You might have an awesome channel banner design, but if the quality is not high enough, it may not look as great as you think once it's placed on your channel. Images on the web should have a resolution of at least 72 dpi. Trust me, it makes all the difference.

When it comes to a profile picture, it should match your channel banner. Since the picture is in such a small space, try not to overload it with anything. One of my first profile pictures tried to cram in the words "SeanViews Season 2. Coming in December." The profile picture was so small you couldn't even read the words. I would suggest putting your face on it instead of a logo or a pattern. I think it adds a more personal touch to your channel's design.

② MAKE A CHANNEL TRAILER

S urprisingly, not many channels on YouTube make trailers. The trailer is the first thing a viewer sees when they stumble upon your channel, and it's a great way to gain new fans quickly. Here are some tips for making your channel trailer: Keep it short! It should be around 20-40 seconds to hold the viewer's attention. You want people to watch the entire thing, right? Use some fun (copyright-free) music and don't take too long to convey why someone should subscribe. Use clips from your previous videos that have lots of action or show something funny happening to match the pace of the music. I would suggest not using any audio from your videos because it may clash with the music in your trailer. Use some animated text to describe to the viewer what kinds of videos you make such as unboxing videos, comedy videos, or challenges, to name a few. Most editing software has some text animations included. When you finish your trailer, watch it back and ask yourself, "Would I subscribe to this channel?" If that answer is yes, you should post it. If it's a no, keep tweaking the final product until it fits your liking. I usually update my channel trailer every few months or so. You can update yours as often as you like. Don't just describe your videos to the viewer, show them.

③ SET UP A FILMING LOCATION

It's always good to have one place where you shoot many of your videos. It helps with building your brand and recognition. It's also good to have one place where you can always keep your camera and lights set up. If you want to shoot a video ASAP, you won't have to spend time setting up and moving all of your equipment. As for the lighting, If you don't have a window with natural light coming in, I would suggest using an umbrella light or ring light for your videos. An umbrella light is usually used when filming with multiple people, a ring light is best used when filming by yourself. The ring light gives nice and even lighting around your face. Just know that it's very bright and can be distracting if you aren't used to it. The umbrella light illuminates anything in it's path. If you have one or two of those, it's very hard to mess up the lighting of your video. You can't go wrong with either.

4 MAKE AN OUTLINE

Nobody wants to watch a video where the person talking does not know what they are going to say next. If you have a good video idea, make an outline of what you want to say in that video so you aren't stuttering or pausing to think every second. In my video titled "AUDITIONING FOR AMERICA'S GOT TALENT!" I wrote an outline of what I was going to say and what the judges were going to say. I wanted to get all of the words exactly right so I wouldn't have to re-shoot any clips.

⑤ STICK TO A VIDEO SCHEDULE

When making videos on YouTube, consistency is key. Your viewers will want to know when to expect a new video from you. They can look forward to it. Even if you can't always commit to a schedule and you post a day late, your viewers will know the general day they can expect a new video. It's better than saying something like "new videos whenever I feel like it." You could either be posting every day, every week, every month, every two months, it could really mean anything. I love knowing when I can expect a new video from my favorite creators.

(6) MAKE A VIDEO INTRO

An intro at the beginning of every video can really help build your brand. If you use the same logo and music enough, people will start to associate it with your channel whenever they see it. Don't make it too loud and busy; make it look as professional as possible. There are even some websites where you can make an intro from a template for free. There are plenty of options for intros; find one that suits you best. Make sure to use one that you like. I have been known to constantly change up my intro. I've tried to keep the same one, but then something new comes along that I like even better. It isn't necessarily a bad thing to change your intro, but it's probably best not to do it too often—maybe once every few months, if you really want to.

COLLAB WITH FRIENDS

C ollabs are a great way to expand your fanbase to others. Even if the person you are making a video with doesn't have a YouTube channel, it still makes the video more interesting. When I did the Pizza Challenge with my sister, it made it more entertaining than if I had done it by myself. Usually, if I have a good video idea or a challenge, I will ask my friend Blake if he wants to film it with me. If you make a video with someone who has a youtube channel, you will be getting more views from the people who are subscribed to the person you collab with. I've discovered many people on YouTube because they did videos with people who I like to watch. This will also benefit the other person. When doing a collab, it's always good to make a video for each channel. That's how you will get their fans, and they will get yours.

⑧ USE TAGS

Tags are something that smaller YouTubers usually don't care about, but they are a great way to get noticed on YouTube. For example, when I made "What to do in a Hotel Room," I added these tags that said things like "Sean, Comedy, Hotel, Room, What, To, Do, In, Funny, YouTuber, Vlog" and many more. Tags are a part of YouTube's algorithm for search results. If I hadn't added any tags to that video, it would have only shown up if someone had searched the exact title of my video. If I add tags relating to every aspect of that video, it will show up in many more search results. However, when adding tags, be truthful. For example, if you made a video called "Eating Pizza" you shouldn't add unrelated tags like "monkey, space, rocket, top 10 music videos." Don't abuse the system. Add as many tags as you can—as long as they relate to your video.

(9) LINK TO OTHER SOCIALS

Either at the end of the video, in the description, or both, you should promote your other social media accounts so your viewers can connect and keep up with you in many places. It's a great way to expand your online presence quickly. On other social media platforms like Twitter, you can get reactions from your fans instantly, unlike when you make a YouTube video. When making a video, you have to edit and post it before you see reactions from fans. If you tweet something, like a question or a poll, you will see instant results

⑩ DON'T SELF PROMOTE IN COMMENTS

T his is a pet peeve of mine. I can't stand it when I see comments like: "Hey this was a great video! Hilarious! I make videos similar to this video every Friday! I'm trying to reach 100 subs by the end of the month!!" I get it, we're all creators, but promote yourself on your own social media accounts, not others'. Don't put spam in other creators' comment sections. Chances are, that won't help you get subscribers. Most people get annoyed by it. I get comments like these pretty regularly. Luckily, YouTube filters most of them out automatically.

THINGS I
wish I knew

11 HAVE ORIGINAL IDEAS

It's always fun to do popular challenges or trends, right? Even though it may seem like a good video, there are plenty of people who have done the same thing on their channels. To stand out, do the challenge but add your own creative spin onto it. For example, I made a video titled "TASTING WEIRD CHIPS WITH MY UNCLE AND SISTER!" This video has been done many times but, did they have a ridiculous uncle doing it also? That still would've been a good video if I did it with my sister alone, but I included my uncle in the video also. He made it 100% more hilarious and ridiculous with the things he was doing throughout the video. That set it apart from similar videos online. When you put your own spin on a popular trend or challenge, that really shows your creativity and isn't that what YouTube's all about? I love watching people make up new challenges or add a twist to old ones. It keeps the video fresh and you won't blend in with everyone else.

12 SPEND TIME EDITING

E diting your video is just as important as filming the video. Not everyone has the attention span to watch someone sit down and quietly talk to the camera. Editing is a good way to keep the viewer watching your video. You can cut out all of the breaths and pauses and just have the content that you want to show the viewer. You can also add some effects and background music. I personally like adding different cuts, zooms, and graphics to my videos to keep the viewer entertained. If you think you have a great video idea, the editing will make or break the video. It could be really funny and fast, or it could be boring and slow. It all depends on the music you use, the amount of cuts you make, and much more. It's a very crucial step in making your videos.

(13) SPEND TIME ON YOUR THUMBNAILS

How often do you click on a video because it had an eye-catching thumbnail? I would guess pretty often. A thumbnail for your video is almost as crucial as the titling of the video. Don't just use a random screenshot from the video, take a picture from an interesting moment, spend time adding a border, some text, or any other effects you think would look good. To know if you have a good thumbnail, take a moment and ask yourself "Would I click on this video?" If the answer is no, keep working until you say yes.

USE COPYRIGHT FREE MUSIC

N ow this is a mistake I have made too many times. When you are looking for intro music or background music, make sure it isn't copyrighted.   Chances are, if you want to use a popular song in your video, you will not be able to make any money off of that video. Even if you are using a version without vocals. I lost count of how many times I had to re-upload videos because I got a copyright claim. If you are partnered with a network, they usually have music you can use for free. If you aren't partnered with anyone, you can use the YouTube audio library. Surprisingly, a lot of creators use it and the music really isn't that bad. If you are unsure about using a certain song for fear of copyright, take the safe route and use the YouTube audio library.

GET TO THE POINT

The first thing you want to do when making a YouTube video is to get your point across, right? That's always a very important part of your content, obviously, but don't make the intro of your video too long. If someone clicks on a video titled "My Daily Makeup Routine" chances are, they don't want to sit through a two minute intro before you start putting on the makeup. If a viewer gets bored, they will leave. That is called "Viewer Abandonment." The amount of time a viewer spends watching your video is always important. You don't want someone to leave in the middle of your video, right? Don't spend too long introducing the video and **get to the point.**

16 DON'T MAKE MULTIPLE CHANNELS

Now this is something that I am definitely guilty of doing when I first started my YouTube channel. I made so many channels that I never posted on. There was SeanViews, SeanViews Random, SeanViews News, SeanViews Extras, Sean Plays, SeanViews Backstage, and many more. I knew I wouldn't be using my other channels because in my first channel trailer I said "I also have a channel called SeanViews News, but don't bother subscribing to that one because I won't put anything on it." Make only one channel and put all of your content on it. If you have fans on your main channel, don't make them move somewhere else for more content.

17 PAY ATTENTION TO LAWS

T his one is very important. If you would like to make a hidden camera public prank video, you need to know if you're allowed to in that area. This can go for stores, cities, or even states. For example, in Philadelphia, Pennsylvania, it's illegal to do hidden camera pranks. If you don't know about these laws, it could get you in some trouble.

(18) IGNORE HATE COMMENTS

This one should be obvious. If you are getting hate comments. don't respond to them. The person writing that comment wants you to respond. They want attention, that's all. If they don't like your video, why are they watching? Just delete the comments and move on. Don't dwell on negative comments, focus on positive comments that you know will support and uplift you. Don't give haters your time. That's the entire reason why they write the comment. With that being said, don't confuse constructive criticism with hate. There is a fine line that divides the two. If someone comments suggesting some things to do better, even if the person says they don't like the video, it would probably be constructive criticism. If they aren't telling you what to change or what's wrong with your channel and they are just hating, don't waste your time.

(19) QUALITY OVER QUANTITY

If you are trying to commit to making a video every week, then that's great! If you can't think of a good video idea for one week, just don't post anything. Not posting a video is better than posting something that you don't like. If you film something but you don't like the way it turned out, don't post it just because you are worried about disappointing your subscribers. Quality over quantity is always a good rule to follow. Your genuine and loyal subscribers will understand.

NUMBERS AREN'T EVERYTHING

When you are making YouTube videos, don't dwell constantly on the amount of subscribers you have. In the long run, it won't matter how many subscribers you had, the only thing that will matter is if you had fun making videos. Even for people who do YouTube as a full time job, don't constantly care about who has more followers or how many subscribers you have gained.

hopefully these tips help you in your YouTube journey.

i know they've helped me ;)

ABOUT THE AUTHOR

Sean Worth is a child of the 21st century with a passion to learn and express himself. Born into a technology rich home, he launched his YouTube channel, SeanViews at the age of 9. In the 5 years following, he has created hundreds of videos featuring technology reviews, unboxings, cooking shows, parodies, and general teen fun for his audience. In his spare time, he produces videos for his school, his church, and special celebrations. He teaches multimedia production, and now has mastered self-publishing.

join the adventure at
SeanViews.com